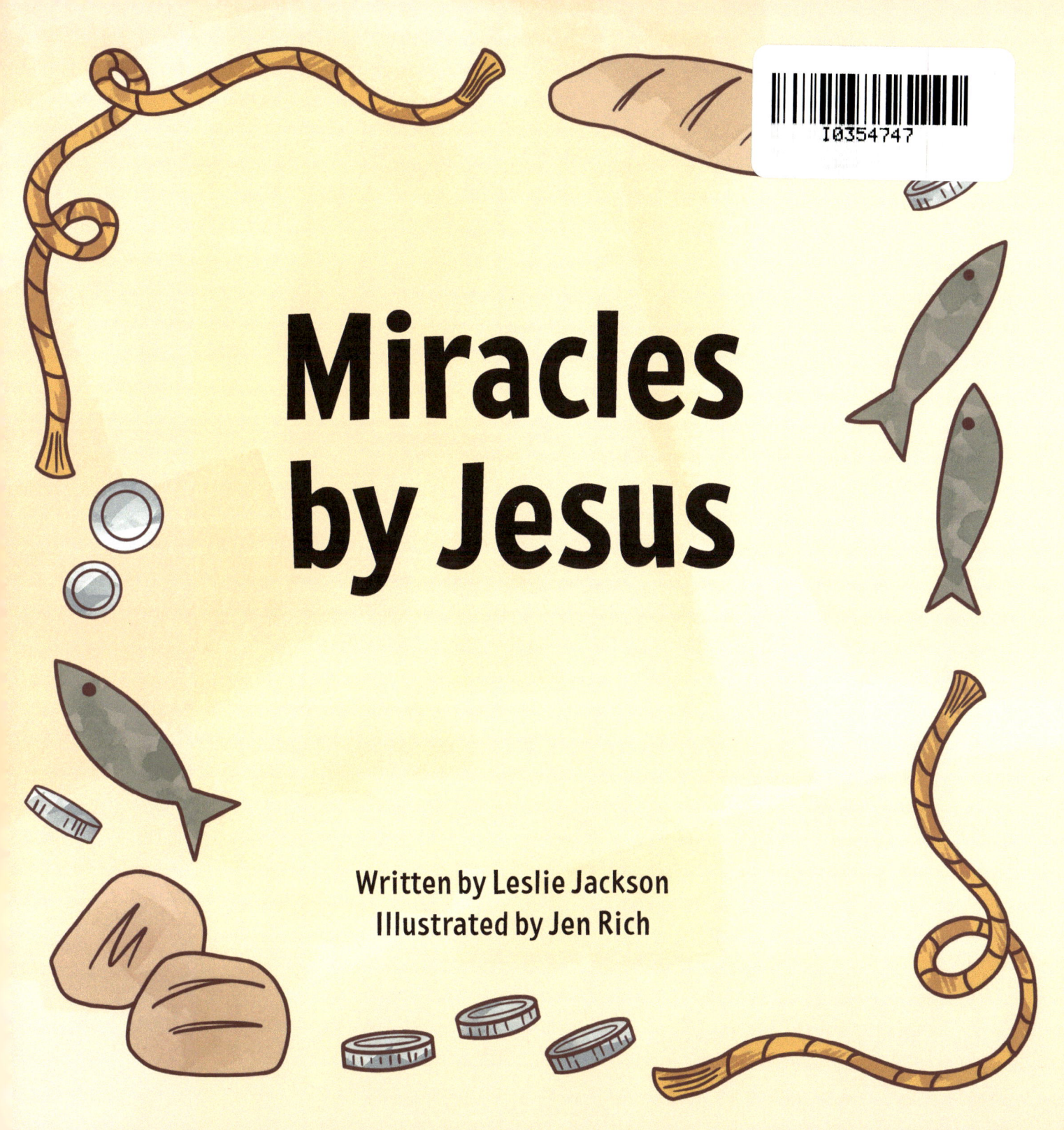

Jesus Uses a Fish to Pay Taxes

Matthew 17:24-27

The tax collector asked Peter, "Does your teacher, Jesus, pay Temple tax?"

Peter said, "Yes, he does." Then he went into the house.

Peter came into the house and Jesus said, "Go fishing and open the mouth of the first fish you catch. In his mouth, you will find the money needed to pay the tax for both of us."

Peter did as Jesus said and found a large silver coin in the fish's mouth. Because of Jesus' miracle, Peter was able to pay the tax with it.

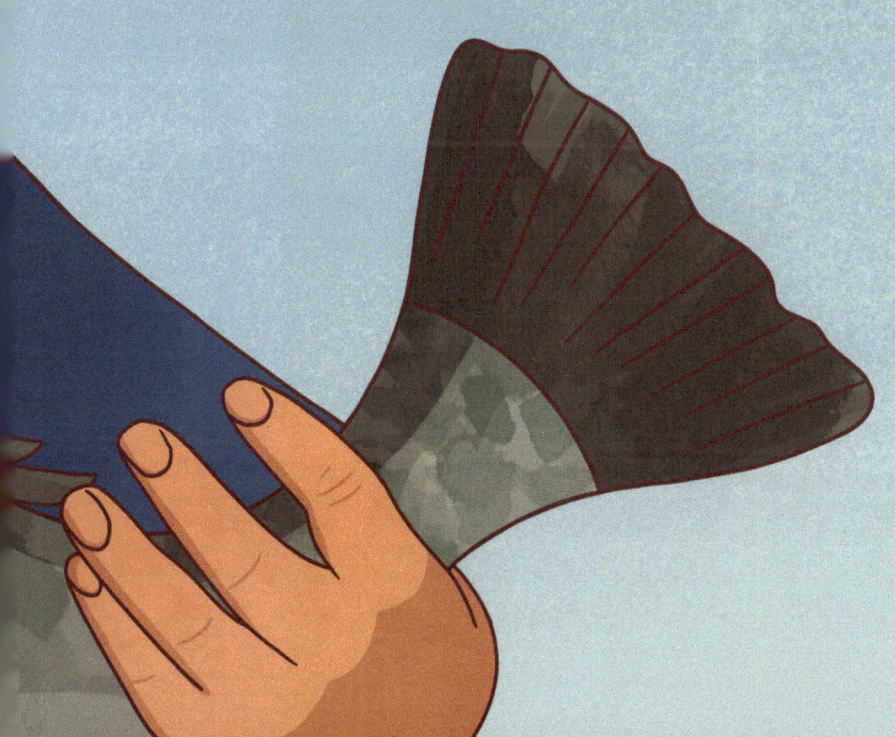

Jesus Heals

Mark 2:1-12

Four men brought their friend on a mat because he could not walk, and they wanted Jesus to heal him.

Because of the large crowd, they could not get in through the door, so they dug a hole in the roof above the head of Jesus.

Then, they lowered their friend on the mat right down in front of Jesus.

Jesus was happy to help, and he made the man well. The healed man, jumped up, grabbed his mat, and walked around praising God!

Jesus Feeds 5,000

Mark 6:32-44

When Jesus went to shore, he saw a great crowd of about 5,000 families.

When it grew late, the people became hungry.

They only had five loaves of bread and two fish for all the people to share.

Jesus had the people sit down on the green grass in groups of 50s and 100s.

With the five loaves and two fish in Jesus' hands, he looked up to Heaven, said a blessing, and He thanked God for providing food for all the people.

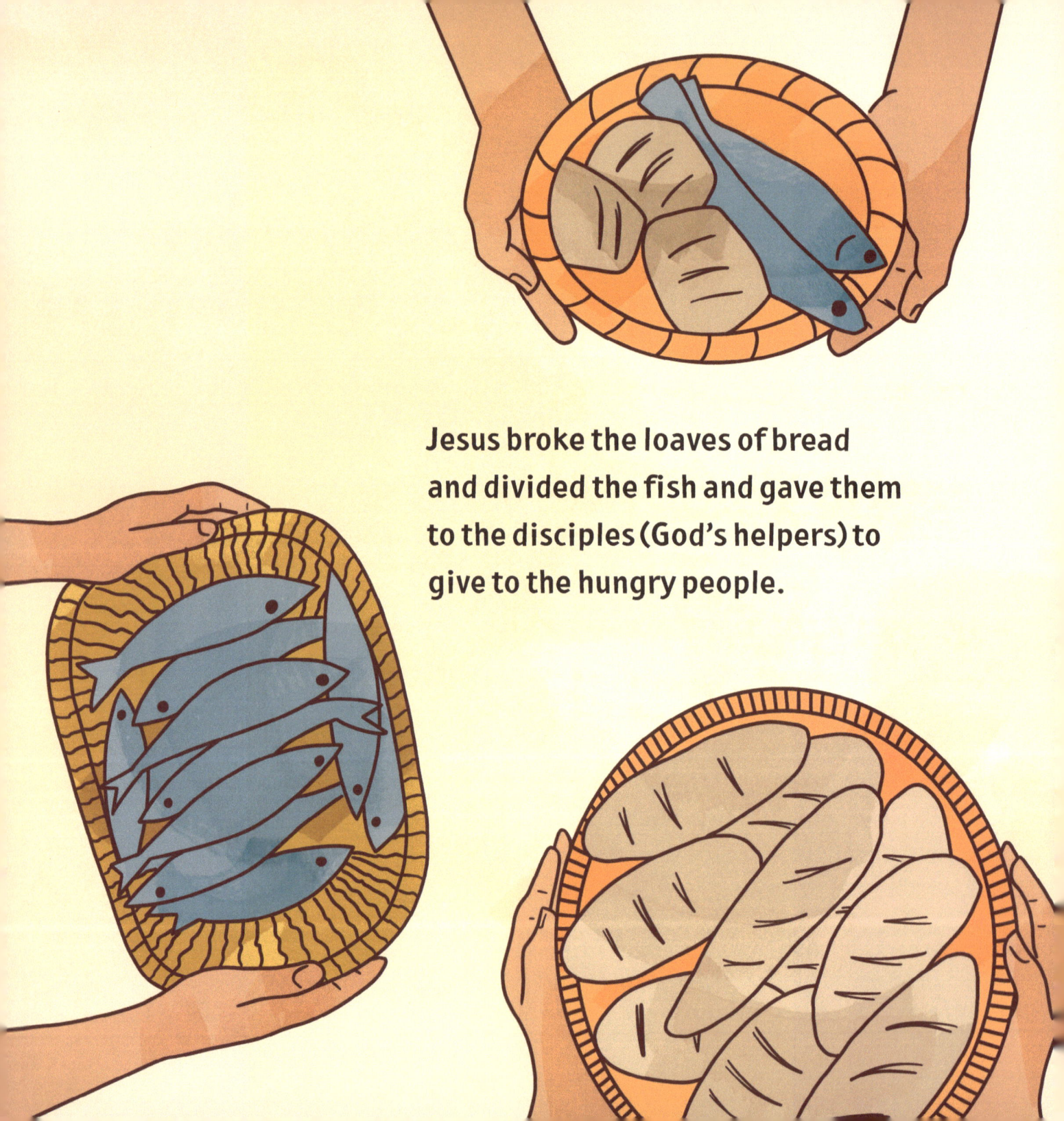

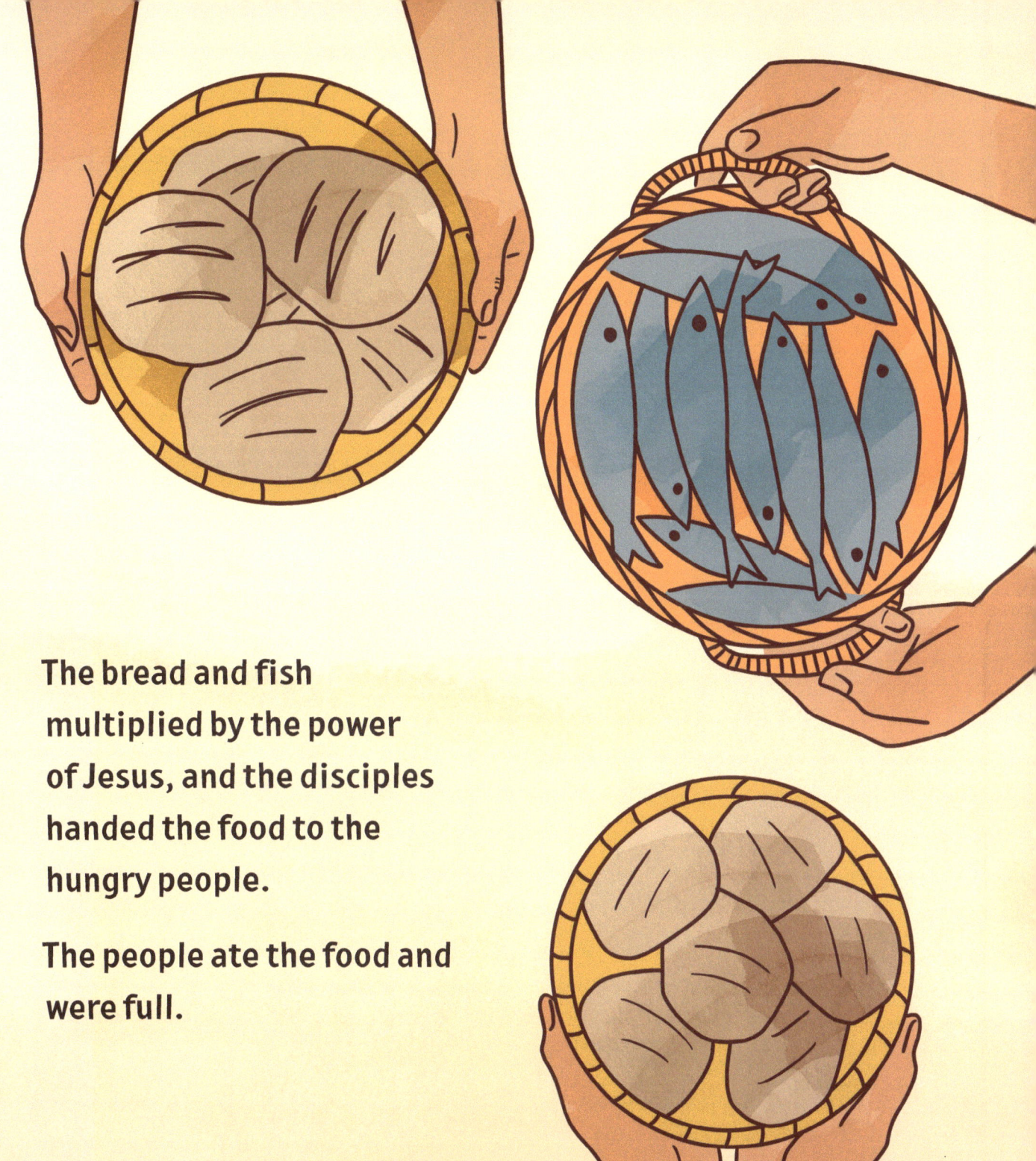

The bread and fish multiplied by the power of Jesus, and the disciples handed the food to the hungry people.

The people ate the food and were full.

After everyone ate the bread and fish, Jesus provided so much food, the disciples picked up the leftovers, and they filled 12 baskets.

Jesus loves you and wants to be your best friend.
Receive Him into your heart by saying this prayer:

Come into my heart, Lord Jesus.
Come in today. Come in to stay.
Come into my heart, Lord Jesus! Amen.

Now, talk to Jesus out loud or in your heart anytime you want, anywhere, and about anything.

Miracles by Jesus

Copyright ©2024 by Leslie Jackson.

All rights reserved. No part of this book may be reproduced in any form or by any means, electronic, or mechanical, including photography, recording, e-books, or any information storage and retrieval system, without permission in writing from the publisher.

ISBN: 978-1-7345854-6-9

Illustrations by Jen Rich
Book Design by Paul Nylander | Illustrada

For more information visit: https://LeslieJackson.org

www.ingramcontent.com/pod-product-compliance
Lightning Source LLC
Chambersburg PA
CBHW041528070526
44585CB00003B/122